William Shakespeare: *Selected Sonnets and Verse*
edited, with an introduction by Mark Tuley

William Shakespeare: *The Sonnets*
edited and introduced by Mark Tuley

*Shakespeare: Love, Poetry and Magic
in Shakespeare's Sonnets and Plays*
by B.D. Barnacle

Edmund Spenser: *Heavenly Love: Selected Poems*
selected and introduced by Teresa Page

Robert Herrick: *Delight In Disorder: Selected Poems*
edited and introduced by M.K. Pace

Sir Thomas Wyatt: *Love For Love: Selected Poems*
selected and introduced by Louise Cooper

John Donne: *Air and Angels: Selected Poems*
selected and introduced by A.H. Ninham

D.H. Lawrence: *Being Alive: Selected Poems*
edited with an introduction by Margaret Elvy

D.H. Lawrence: Symbolic Landscapes
by Jane Foster

D.H. Lawrence: Infinite Sensual Violence
by M.K. Pace

Percy Bysshe Shelley: *Paradise of Golden Lights: Selected Poems*
selected and introduced by Charlotte Greene

Thomas Hardy: *Her Haunting Ground: Selected Poems*
edited, with an introduction by A.H. Ninham

Sexing Hardy: Thomas Hardy and Feminism
by Margaret Elvy

Emily Bronte: *Darkness and Glory: Selected Poems*
selected and introduced by Miriam Chalk

John Keats: *Bright Star: Selected Poems*
edited with an introduction by Miriam Chalk

Henry Vaughan: *A Great Ring of Pure and Endless Light: Selected Poems*
selected and introduced by A.H. Ninham

The Crescent Moon Book of Love Poetry
edited by Louise Cooper

The Crescent Moon Book of Mystical Poetry in English
edited by Carol Appleby

The Crescent Moon Book of Nature Poetry From Langland to Lawrence
edited by Margaret Elvy

The Crescent Moon Book of Metaphysical Poetry
edited and introduced by Charlotte Greene

The Crescent Moon Book of Elizabethan Love Poetry
edited and introduced by Carol Appleby

The Crescent Moon Book of Romantic Poetry
edited and introduced by L.M. Poole

Blinded By Her Light The Love-Poetry of Robert Graves
by Jeremy Mark Robinson

The Best of Peter Redgrove's Poetry: The Book of Wonders
by Peter Redgrove, edited and introduced by Jeremy Mark Robinson

Peter Redgrove: Here Comes the Flood
by Jeremy Mark Robinson

Sex-Magic-Poetry-Cornwall: A Flood of Poems
by Peter Redgrove, edited with an essay by Jeremy Mark Robinson

Brigitte's Blue Heart
by Jeremy Reed

Claudia Schiffer's Red Shoes
by Jeremy Reed

By-Blows: Uncollected Poems
by D.J. Enright

Petrarch, Dante and the Troubadours: The Religion of Love and Poetry
by Cassidy Hughes

Dante: *Selections From the Vita Nuova*
translated by Thomas Okey

Arthur Rimbaud: *Selected Poems*
edited and translated by Andrew Jary

Paradise of Golden Lights
Selected Poems

Paradise of Golden Lights
Selected Poems

Percy Bysshe Shelley

Edited by Charlotte Greene

CRESCENT MOON

CRESCENT MOON PUBLISHING
P.O. Box 1312, Maidstone
Kent, ME14 5XU
Great Britain, www.crmoon.com

First published 1994. Second edition 2008. Revised 2016.
Introduction © Charlotte Greene, 1994, 2008,2016.

Printed and bound in the U.S.A..
Set in Garamond Book 12 on 15pt.
Designed by Radiance Graphics.

British Library Cataloguing in Publication data

Shelley, Percy Bysshe, 1792-1822
Paradise of Golden Lights: Selected Poems. – 2nd ed. (British Poets Series)
I. Title II. Greene, Charlotte
III. Series
821.7

ISBN-13 9781861711809
ISBN-13 9781861715340

CONTENTS

TO A SKYLARK

HAIL TO thee, blithe Spirit!
  Bird thou never wert,
That from heaven, or near it,
  Pourest thy full heart
In profuse strains of unpremeditated art.

Higher still and higher
  From the earth thou springest
Like a cloud of fire;
  The blue deep thou wingest,
And singing still dost soar, and soaring ever singest.

In the golden lightning
  Of the sunken sun,
O'er which clouds are bright'ning,
  Thou dost float and run;
Like an unbodied joy whose race is just begun.

The pale purple even
  Melts around thy flight;
Like a star of heaven,
  In the broad daylight
Thou art unseen, but yet I hear thy shrill delight,

Keen as are the arrows
  Of that silver sphere,
Whose intense lamp narrows

In the white dawn clear
Until we hardly see – we feel that it is there.

All the earth and air
With thy voice is loud,
As, when night is bare,
    From one lonely cloud
The moon rains out her beams, and
    Heaven is overflowed.

What thou art we know not;
    What is most like thee?
From rainbow clouds there flow not
    Drops so bright to see
As from thy presence showers a rain of melody.

Like a Poet hidden
    In the light of thought,
Singing hymns unbidden,
    Till the world is wrought
To sympathy with hopes and fears it heeded not:

Like a high-born maiden
    In a palace-tower,
Soothing her love-laden
    Soul in secret hour
With music sweet as love, which overflows her bower

Like a glow-worm golden
    In a dell of dew,
Scattering unbeholden
    Its aëreal hue
Among the flowers and grass, which screen it from

the view!
Like a rose embowered
  In its own green leaves,
By warm winds deflowered,
  Till the scent it gives
Makes faint with too much sweet those heavy-
              wingèd thieves:

Sound of vernal showers
  On the twinkling grass,
Rain-awakened flowers,
  All that ever was
Joyous, and clear, and fresh, thy music doth surpass:

Teach us, Sprite or Bird,
  What sweet thoughts are thine:
I have never heard
  Praise of love or wine
That panted forth a flood of rapture so divine.

Chorus Hymeneal,
  Or triumphal chant,
Matched with thine would be all
  But an empty vaunt,
A thing wherein we feel there is some hidden want.

What objects are the fountains
  Of thy happy strain?
What fields, or waves, or mountains?
  What shapes or sky or plain?
What love of thine own kind? what ignorance of pain?

With thy clear keen joyance
   Languor cannot be:
Shadow of annoyance
   Never came near thee:
Thou lovest – but ne'er knew love's sad satiety.

Waking or asleep,
   Thou of death must deem
Things more true and deep
   Than we mortals dream,
Or how could thy notes flow in such a crystal stream?

We look before and after,
   And pine for what is not:
Our sincerest laughter
   With some pain is fraught;
Our sweetest songs are those that tell of saddest
                      thought.

Yet if we could scorn
   Hate, and pride, and fear;
If we were things born
   Not to shed a tear,
I know not how thy joy we ever should come near.

Better than all measures
   Of delightful sound,
Better than all treasures
   That in books are found,
Thy skill to poet were, thou scorner of the ground!

Teach me half the gladness
   That thy brain must know,

Such harmonious madness
    From my lips would flow
The world should listen then – as I am listening now.

A LAMENT

I

O WORLD! O life! O time!
On whose last steps I climb,
    Trembling at that where I had stood before;
When will return the glory of your prime?
            No more! Oh, nevermore!

II

Out of the day and night
A joy has taken flight;
    Fresh spring, and summer, and winter hoar,
Move my faint heart with grief, but with delight
            No more – Oh, never more!

ODE TO THE WEST WIND

I

O WILD West wind, thou breath of Autumn's being,
Thou, from whose unseen presence the leaves
                                     dead
Are driven, like ghosts from an enchanter fleeing,

Yellow, and black, and pale, and hectic red,
Pestilence-stricken multitudes: O thou,
Who chariotest to their dark wintry bed

The wingèd seeds, where they lie cold and low,
Each like a corpse within its grave, until
Thine azure sister of the Spring shall blow

Her clarion o'er the dreaming earth, and fill
(Driving sweet buds like flocks to feed in air)
With living hues and odours plain and hill:

Wild spirit, which art moving everywhere;
Destroyer and preserver; hear, oh, hear!

II

Thou on whose stream, mid the steep sky's
                            commotion,

Loose clouds like earth's decaying leaves are shed,
Shook from the tangled boughs of Heaven and
                                    Ocean,

Angels of rain and lightning: there are spread
On the blue surface of thine aëry surge,
Like the bright hair uplifted from the head

Of some fierce Maenad, even from the dim verge
Of the horizon to the zenith's height,
The locks of the approaching storm. Thou dirge

Of the dying year, to which this closing night
Will be the dome of a vast sepulchre,
Vaulted with all thy congregated might

Of vapours, from whose solid atmosphere
Black rain, and fire, and hail will burst: oh, hear!

III

Thou who didst waken from his summer dreams
The blue Mediterranean, where he lay,
Lulled by the coil of his crystalline streams,

Beside a pumice isle in Baiae's bay,
And saw in sleep old palaces and towers
Quivering within the wave's intenser day,

All overgrown with azure moss and flowers
So sweet, the sense faints picturing them! Thou
For whose path the Atlantic's level powers

Cleave themselves into chasms, while far below
The sea blooms and the oozy woods which wear
The sapless foliage of the ocean, know

Thy voice, and suddenly grow gray with fear,
And tremble and despoil themselves; oh, hear!

IV

If I were a dead leaf thou mightest bear;
If I were a swift cloud to fly with thee;
A wave to pant beneath thy power, and share

The impulse of thy strength, only less free
Than thou, O uncontrollable! if even
I were as in my boyhood, and could be

The comrade of thy wanderings over heaven,
As then, when to outstrip thy skiey speed
Scarce seemed a vision; I would ne'er have striven

As thus with thee in prayer in my sore need
Oh, lift me as a wave, a leaf, a cloud!
I fall upon the thorns of life! I bleed!

A heavy weight of hours has chained and bowed
One too like thee: tameless, and swift, and proud.

V

Make me thy lyre, even as the forest is:
What if my leaves are falling like its own!
The tumult of thy mighty harmonies

Will take from both a deep, autumnal tone,
Sweet though in sadness. Be thou, Spirit fierce,
My spirit! Be thou me, impetuous one!

Drive my dead thoughts over the universe
Like withered leaves to quicken a new birth!
And, by the incantation of this verse,

Scatter, as from an unextinguished hearth
Ashes and sparks, my words among mankind!
Be through my lips to unawakened earth

The trumpet of a prophecy! O, Wind,
If Winter comes, can Spring be far behind?

from THE REVOLT OF ISLAM

Canto XII

XXXIII

TILL DOWN that might stream, dark, calm, and fleet,
   Between a chasm of cedarn mountains riven,
Chased by the thronging winds whose viewless
                              feet
   As swift as twinkling beams, had, under Heaven,
   From woods and waves wild sounds and
                              odours driven
The boat fled visibly – three nights and days,
   Borne like a cloud through morn, and noon,
                              and even,
We sailed along the winding watery ways
Of the vast stream, a long and labyrinthine maze.

XXXIV

A scene of joy and wonder to behold
   That river's shapes and shadows changing
                              ever,
   When the broad sunrise filled with deepening gold
   Its whirlpools, where all hues did spread and
                              quiver;

And where melodious falls did burst and shiver
Among rocks clad with flowers, the foam and
spray
Sparkled like stars upon the sunny river,
Or when the moonlight poured a holier day,
One vast and glittering lake around green islands
lay.

XXV

Morn, noon, and even, that boat of pearl outran
The streams which bore it, like the arrowy cloud
Of tempest, or the speedier though of man,
Which flieth forth and cannot make abode;
Sometimes through forests, deep like night, we
glode,
Between the walls of mighty mountains crowned
With Cyclopean piles, whose turrets proud,
The homes of the departed, dimly frowned
O'er the bright waves which girt their dark
foundations round.

XXXVI

Sometimes between the wide and flowering
meadows,
Mile after mile we sailed, and 'twas delight
To see far off the sunbeams chase the shadows
Over the grass; sometimes beneath the night
Of wide and vaulted caves, whose roofs were
bright

With starry gems, we fled, whilst from their deep
 And dark-green chasms, shades beautiful and
  white,
Amid sweet sounds across our path would sweep,
Like swift and lovely dreams that walk the waves of
  sleep.

XXXVII

And ever as we sailed, our minds were full
 Of love and wisdom, which would overflow
In converse wild, and sweet, and wonderful,
 And in quick smiles whose light would come
  and go
Like music o'er wide waves, and in the flow
Of sudden tears, and in the mute caress -
 For a deep shade was cleft, and we did know,
 That virtue, though obscured on Earth, not less
Survives all mortal change in lasting loveliness.

XXXVIII

Three days and nights we sailed, as thought and
  feeling
 Number delightful hours - for through the sky
The spherèd lamps of day and night, revealing
 New changes and new glories, rolled on high,
 Sun, Moon, and moonlike lamps, the progeny
Of a diviner heaven, serene and fair:
 On the fourth day, wild as a windwrought sea
The stream became, and fast and faster bare

The spirit-wingèd boat, steadily speeding there.

XXXIX

   Steady and swift, where the waves rolled like
                    mountains
    Within the vast ravine, whose rifts did pour
  Tumultuous floods from their tend thousand
                    fountains,
    The thunder of whose earth-uplighting roar
    Made the air sweep in whirlwinds from the
                    shore,
  Calm as a shade, the boat of that fair child
    Securely fled, that rapid stress before,
  Amid the topmost spray, and sunbrows wild,
Wreathed in the silver mist; in joy and pride we
                    smiled.

XL

   The torrent of that wide and raging river
    Is passed, and our aëral speed suspended.
  We look behind; a golden mist did quiver
    Where its wild surges with the lake were
                    blended, –
    Our bark hung there, as on a line suspended
  Between two heavens, – that windless waveless
                    lake
    Which four great cataracts from four vales,
                    attended
  By mists, aye feed; from rocks and clouds they

                                                break,
And of that azure sea a silent refuge make.

XLI

   Motionless resting on the lake awhile,
      I saw its marge of snow-bright mountains rear
   Their peaks aloft, I saw each radiant isle,
      And in the midst, afar, even like a sphere
      Hung in one hollow sky, did there appear
   The Temple of the Spirit; on the sound
      Which issued thence, drawn nearer and more
                                                near,
   Like the swift moon this glorious earth around,
The charmèd boat approached, and there its
                                    haven found.

from ADONAIS

IX

OH, WEEP for Adonais! – The quick Dreams,
The passion-wingèd Minisiters of thought,
Who were his flocks, whom near the living streams
Of his young spirit he fed, and whom he taught
The love which was its music, wander not, –
Wander no more, from kindling brain to brain,
But droop there, whence they sprung; and mourn
                                  their lot
Round the cold heart, where, after their sweet pain,
They ne'er will gather strength, or find a home again.

XXVI

'Stay yet awhile! speak to me once again;
Kiss me, so long but as a kiss may live;
And in my heartless breast and burning brain
That word, that kiss, shall all thoughts else survive,
With food of saddest memory kept alive,
Now thou art dead, as if it were a part
Of thee, my Adonais! I would give
All that I am to be as thou now art!
But I am chained to Time, and cannot thence
                                  depart!

XXXIII

His head was bound with pansies overblown,
And faded violets, white, and pied, and blue;
And a light spear topped with a cypress cone,
Round whose rude shaft dark ivy-tresses grew
Yet dripping with the forest's noonday dew,
Vibrated, as the ever-beating heart
Shook the weak hand that grasped it; of that crew
He came the last, neglected and apart;
A herd-abandoned deer struck by the hunter's dart.

XLII

He is made one with Nature: there is heard
His voice in all her music, from the moan
Of thunder, to the song of night's sweet bird;
He is a presence to be felt and known
In darkness and in light, from herb and stone,
Spreading itself where'er that power may move
Which has withdrawn his being to its own;
Which wields the world with never-wearied love,
Sustains it from beneath,a and kindles it above.

LII

The One remains, the many change and pass;
Heaven's light forever shines, Earth's shadows fly;
Life, like a dome of many-coloured glass,
Stains the white radiance of Eternity,
Until death tramples it to fragments. – Die,

If thou would'st be with that which thou dost seek!
Follow where all is fled! – Rome's azure sky,
Flowers, ruins, statues, music, words, are weak
The glory they transfuse with fitting truth to speak.

from PROMETHEUS UNBOUND

Prometheus: MONARCH OF Gods and Daemons, and
                                        all Spirits
But One, who throng those bright and rolling worlds
Which Thou and I alone of living things
Behold with sleepless eyes! regard this Earth
Made multitudinous with thy slaves, whom thou
Requitest for knee-worship, prayer, and praise,
And toil, and hecatombs of broken hearts,
With fear and self-contempt and barren hope.
Whilst me, who am thy foe, eyeless in hate,
Hast thou made reign and triumph, to thy scorn,
O'er mine own misery and thy vain revenge.
Three thousand years of sleep-unsheltered hours,
And moments aye divided by keen pangs
Till they seemed years, torture and solitude,
Scorn and despair, – these are mine empire: –
More glorious far than that which thou surveyest
From thine unenvied throne, O Mighty God!
Almighty, had I deigned to share the shame
Of thine ill tyranny, and hung not here
Nailed to the wall of eagle-baffling mountain,
Black, wintry, dead, unmeasured; without herb,
Insect, or beast, or shape or sound of life.
Ah me! alas, pain, pain ever, for ever!

No change, no pause, no hope! Yet I endure.
I ask the Earth, have not the mountains felt?

I ask yon heaven, the all-beholding Sun,
Has it not seen? The Sea, in storm or calm,
Heaven's ever-changing Shadow, spread below,
Have its deaf waves not heard my agony?
Ah me! alas, pain, pain ever, for ever!

The crawling glaciers pierce me with the spears
Of their moon-freezing crystals, the bright chains
Eat with their burning cold into my bones.
Heaven's wingèd hound, polluting from thy lips
His beak in poison not his own, tears up
My heart; and shapeless sights come wandering by,
The ghastly people of the realm of dream,
Mocking me: and the Earthquake-fiends are
                                     charged
To wrench the rivets from my quivering wounds
When the rocks spilt and close again behind:
While from their loud abysses howling throng
The genii of the storm, urging the rage
Of whirlwind, and afflict me with keen hail.
And yet to me welcome is day and night,
Whether one breaks the hoar frost of the morn,
Or starry, dim, and slow, the other climbs
The leaden-coloured east; for then they lead
The wingless, crawling hours, one among whom
– As some dark Priest hales the reluctant victim
Shall drag thee, cruel king, to kiss the blood
From these pale feet, which then might trample
                                     thee
If they disdained not such a prostrate slave.
Disdain! Ah no! I pity thee. What ruin
Will haunt thee undefended through wide heaven!
How will thy soul, cloven to its depth with terror,

Gape like a hell within! I speak in grief,
Not exultation, for I hate no more,
As then ere misery made me wise. The curse
Once breathed on thee I would recall. Ye Mountains,
Whose many-voicèd Echoes, through the mist
Of cataracts, flung the thunder of that spell!
Ye icy Springs, stagnant with wrinkling frost,
Which vibrated to hear me, and then crept
Shuddering through India! Thou serenest Air,
Through which the Sun walks burning without beams!
And ye swift Whirlwinds, who on poisèd wings
Hung mute And moveless o'er yon hushed abyss,
As thunder, louder than your own, made rock
The orbèd world! If then my words had power,
Though I am changed so that aught evil wish
Is dead within; although no memory be
Of what is hate; let them not lose it now!
What was that curse? for ye all heard me speak.

•

Asia: From all the blasts of heaven thou hast
                              descended:
Yes, like a spirit, like a thought, which makes
Unwonted tears throng to the horny eyes,
And beatings haunt the desolated heart,
Which should have learnt repose: thou hast
                              descended
Cradled in tempests; thou dost wake, O Spring!
O child of many winds! As suddenly
Thou comest as the memory of a dream,
Which now is sad because it hath been sweet;
Like genius, or like joy which riseth up

As from the earth, clothing with golden clouds
The desert of our life.
This is the season, this the day, the hour;
At sunrise thou shouldst come, sweet sister mine,
Too long desired, too long delaying, come!
How like death-worms the wingless moments crawl!
The point of one white star is quivering still
Deep in the orange light of widening morn
Beyond the purple mountains: through a chasm
Of wind-divided mist the darker lake
Reflects it: now it wanes: it gleams again
As the waves fade, and as the burning threads
Of woven cloud unravel in pale air:
'Tis lost! and through yon peaks of cloud-like snow
The roseate sunlight quivers: hear I not
The Æolian music of her sea-green plumes
Winnowing the crimson dawn?

•

Panthea:...I saw not, heard not, moved not, only felt
His presence flow and mingle through my blood
Till it became his life, and his grew mine,
And I was thus absorbed, until it passed,
And like the vapours when the sun sinks down,
Gathering again in drops upon the pines,
And tremulous as they, in the deep night
My being was condensed...
I always knew what I desired before,
Nor ever found delight to wish in vain.
But now I cannot tell thee what I seek;
Even to desire; it is thy sport, false sister;
Thou hast discovered some enchantment old,

Whose spells have stolen my spirit as I slept
And mingled it with thine: for when just now
We kissed, I felt within thy parted lips
The sweet air that sustained me, and the warmth
Of the life-blood, for loss of which I faint,
Quivered between our intertwining arms,

●

Asia: Fit throne for such a power! Magnificent!
How glorious art thou, Earth! And if thou be
The shadow of some spirit lovelier still,
Thou evil stain its work, and it should be
Like its creation, weak yet beautiful,
I could fall down and worship that and thee.
Even now my heart adoreth: Wonderful!
Look, sister, ere the vapour dim thy brain:
Beneath is a wide plain of billowy mist,
As a lake, paving in the morning sky,
With azure waves which burst in silver light,
Some Indian vale. Behold it, rolling on
Under the curdling winds, and is landing
The peak whereon we stand, midway around,
Encinctured by the dark and blooming forests,
Dim twilight-lawns, and stream-illuminèd caves,
And wind-enchanted shapes of wandering mist;
And far on high the keen sky-cleaving mountains
From icy spires of sun-like radiance fling
The dawn, as lifted ocean's dazzling spray,
From some Atlantic islet scattered up,
Spangles the wind with lamp-like water-drops.
The vale is girdled with their walls, a howl
Of cataracts from their thaw-cloven ravines,

Satiates the listening wind, continuous, vast,
Awful as silence. Hark! the rushing snow!
The sun-awakened avalanche! whose mass,
Thrice sifted by the storm, had gathered there
Flake after flake, in heaven-defying minds
As thought by thought is piled, till some great truth
Is loosened, and the nations echo round,
Shaken to their rots, as do the mountains now.

•

Panthea. And from a star upon its forehead, shoot,
Like swords of azure fire, or golden spears
With tyrant-quelling myrtle overtwined,
Embleming heaven and earth united now,
Vast beams like spokes of some invisible wheel
Which whirl as the orb whirls, swifter than thought,
Filling the abyss with sun-like lightenings,
And perpendicular now, and now transverse,
Pierce the dark soil, And as they pierce and pass,
Make bare the secrets of the earth's deep heart;
Infinite mines of adamant and gold,
Valueless stones,a and unimagined gems,
And caverns on crystalline columns poised
With vegetable silver overspread;
Wells of unfathomed fire, and water springs
Whence the great sea, even as a child is fed,
Whose vapours clothe earth's monarch mountain-
                                    tops
With kingly, ermine snow.

•

The Moon As in the soft and sweet eclipse,
    When soul meets soul on lover's lips,
High hearts are calm, and brightest eyes are dull;
    So when thy shadow falls on me,
    Then am I mute and still, by thee
Covered; of thy love, Orb most beautiful,
        Full, oh, too full!

    Thou are speeding round the sun
    Brightest world of many a one;
    Green and azure sphere which shinest
    With a light which is divinest
    Among all the lamps of Heaven
    To whom life and light is given;
    I, thy crystal paramour
    Borne beside thee by a power
    Like the polar Paradise,
    Magnet-like of lovers' eyes;
    I, a most enamoured maiden
    Whose weak brain is overladen
    With the pleasure of her love,
    Maniac-like around thee move
    Gazing, an satiate bride,
    On thy form from every side
    Like a Maenad, round the cup
    Which Agave lifted up
    In the weird Cadmæan forest.
    Brother, wheresoe'er thou soarest
    I must hurry, whirl and follow
    Through the heavens wide and hollow,
    Sheltered by the warm embrace
    Of thy soul from hungry space,

Drinking from thy sense and sight
Beauty, majesty, and might,
As a lover or a chameleon
Grows like what it looks upon,
As a violet's gentle eye
Gazes its hue grows like what it beholds,
As a gray and watery mist
Glows like solid amethyst
Athwart the western mountain it enfolds,
When the sunset sleeps
Upon its snow.

HYMN TO INTELLECTUAL BEAUTY

I

THE AWFUL shadow of some unseen Power
 Floats though unseen among us, visiting
 This various world with as inconstant wing
As summer winds that creep from lower to flower, –
Like moonbeams that behind some piny mountain
        shower,
  It visits with inconstant glance
  Each human heart and countenance;
Like hues and harmonies of evening, –
  Like clouds in starlight widely spread, –
  Like memory of music fled, –
  Like aught that for its grace may be
Dear, and yet dearer for its mystery.

II

Spirit of Beauty, that dost consecrate
 With thine own hues all thou dost shine upon
 Of human thought or form, – where art thou
        gone?
Why dost thou pas away and leave our state,
This dim vast vale of tears, vacant and desolate?
  Ask why the sunlight not for ever
  Weaves rainbows o'er yon mountain-river,

Why aught should fail and fade that once is shown,
    Why fear and dream and death and birth
    Cast on the daylight of this earth
    Such gloom, – why man has such a scope
For love and hate, despondency and hope?

III

No voice from some sublimer world hath ever
  To sage or poet these responses given –
  Therefore the names of Demon, Ghost, and
                           Heaven,
Remain the records of their vain endeavour,
Frail spells – whose uttered charm might not avail to
                           sever,
    From all we hear and all we see,
    Doubt, chance, and mutability.
Thy light alone – like mist o'er mountains driven,
    Or music by the night-wind sent
    Through strings of some still instrument,
    Or moonlight on a midnight stream,
Gives grace and truth to life's unquiet dream.

IV

Love, hope, and Self-esteem, like clouds depart
  And come, for some uncertain moments lent.
  Man were immortal, and omnipotent,
Didst thou, unknown and awful as thou art,
Keep with thy glorious train firm state within his heart.
    Thou messenger of sympathies,

That wax and wane in lovers' eyes –
Thou – that to human thought art nourishment,
    Like darkness to a dying flame!
    Depart not as thy shadow came,
    Depart not – lest the grave should be,
Like life and fear, a dark reality.

V

While yet a boy I sought, for ghosts, and sped
    Through many a listening chamber, cave and ruin,
    And straight wood, with fearful steps pursuing
Hopes of high talk with the departed dead.
I called on poisonous names with which our youth is
                                 fed;
    I was not heard – I saw them not –
    When musing deeply on the lot
Of life, at that sweet time when winds are wooing
    All vital things that wake to bring
    News of birds and blossoming, –
    Sudden, thy shadow fell on me;
I shrieked, and clasped my hands in ecstasy!

VI

I vowed that I would dedicate my powers
    To thee and thine – have I not kept the vow?
    With beating heart and streaming eyes, even now
I call the phantoms of a thousand hours
Each from his voiceless grave: they have in visioned
                     bowers

Of studious zeal or love's delight
Outwatched with me the envious night –
They know that never joy illumined my brow
    Unlinked with hope that thou wouldst free
    This world from its dark slavery,
    That thou – O awful Loveliness,
Wouldst give whate'er these words cannot express.

VII

The day more solemn and serene
    When noon is past – there is a harmony
    In autumn, and a lustre in its sky,
Which through the summer is not heard or seen,
As if it could not be, as if it had not been!
    Thus let thy power, which like the truth
    Of nature of my passive youth
Descended, to my onward life supply
    Its calm – to one who worships thee,
    And every form containing thee,
    Whom, Spirit fair, thy spells did bind
To fear himself, and love all human kind.

ODE TO HEAVEN

CHORUS OF SPIRITS

First Spirit

PALACE-ROOF of cloudless nights!
Paradise of golden lights!
   Deep, immeasurable, vast,
Which art now, and which wert then
   Of the Present and the Past,
Of the eternal Where and When,
   Presence-chamber, temple, home,
   Ever-canopying dome,
   Of acts and ages yet to come!

Glorious shapes have life in thee,
   Earth, and all earth's company;
   Living globes which ever throng
Thy deep chasms ad wildernesses;
   And green worlds that glide along;
And swift stars with flashing tresses;
   And icy moons most cold and bright,
   And mighty suns beyond the night,
   Atoms of intensest light.

Even thy name is as a god,
Heaven! for thou art the abode

Of that Power which is the glass
Wherein man his nature sees.
    Generations as they pass
Worship thee with bended knees.
    Their unremaining gods and they
    Like a river roll away:
    Thou remainest such – alway! –

Second Spirit

Thou art but the mind's first chamber,
Round which its young fancies clamber,
    Like weak insects in a cave,
Lighted up by stalactites;
    But the portal of the grave,
Where a world of new delights
    Will make thy best glories seem
    But a dim and noonday gleam
    From the shadow of a dream!

Third Spirit

Peace! the abyss is wreathed with scorn
At your presumption, atom-born!
    What is Heaven? and what are ye
Who its brief expanse inherit?
    What are suns and spheres which flee
    With the instinct of that Spirit
    Of which ye are but a part?
    Drops which Nature's mighty heart
Drives through thinnest veins! Depart!

What is Heaven? a globe of dew,
Filling in the morning new
   Some eyed flower whose young leaves waken
On an unimagined world:
   Constellated suns unshaken,
Orbits measureless, are furled
    In that frail and fading sphere,
    With ten millions gathered there,
    To tremble, gleam, and disappear.

LOVE'S PHILOSOPHY

I

THE FOUNTAINS mingle with the river
   And the rivers with the Ocean,
The winds of heaven mix for ever
   With a sweet emotion;
Nothing in the world is single;
   All things by a law divine
In one spirit meet and mingle.
   Why not I with thine? –

II

See the mountains kiss high Heaven
   And the waves clasp one another;
No sister-flower would be forgiven
   If it disdained its brother;
And the sunlight clasps the earth
   And the moonbeams kiss the sea:
What is all this sweet work worth
   If thou kiss not me?

THE CLOUD

I BRING fresh showers for the thirsting flowers,
    From the seas and the streams;
I bear light shade for the leaves when laid
    In their noonday dreams.
From my wings are shaken the dews that waken
    The sweet buds every one,
When rocked to rest on their mother's breast,
    As she dances about the sun,
I wield the flail of the lashing hail,
    And whiten the green plains under,
And then again I dissolve it in rain,
    And laugh as I pass in thunder.

I sift the snow on the mountains below,
    And their great pines groan aghast;
And all the night 'tis my pillow white,
    While I sleep in the arms of the blast.
Sublime on the towers of my skiey bowers,
    Lightning my pilot sits;
In a cavern under is fettered the thunder,
    It struggles and howls at fits;
Over earth and ocean, with gentle motion,
    This pilot is guiding me,
Lured by the love of the genii that move
  In the depths of the purple sea;
Over the rills,a and the crags, and the hills,
  Over the lakes and the plains,

Wherever he dream, under mountain or stream,
    The Spirit he loves remains;
And I all the while bask in Heaven's blue smile,
    Whilst he is dissolving in rains.

The sanguine Sunrise, with his meteor eyes,
    And his burning plumes outspread,
Leaps on the back of my sailing rack,
    When the morning star shines dead;
As on the jag of a mountain crag,
    Which an earthquake rocks and swings,
An eagle alit one moment may sit
    In the light of its golden wings.
And when Sunset may breathe, from the lit sea
                    beneath,
    Its ardours of rest and of love,
And the crimson pall of eve may fall
    From the depth of heaven above,
With wings folded I rest, on mine aëry nest,
    As still as a brooding dove.

That orbèd maiden with white fire laden,
    Whom mortals call the Moon,
Glides glimmering o'er my fleece-like floor,
    By the midnight breezes strewn;
And wherever the beat of her unseen feet,
    Which only the angels hear,
May have broken the woof of my tent's thin roof,
    The stars peep behind her and peer;
And I laugh to see them whirl and flee,
    Like a swarm of golden bees,
When I widen the rent in the wind-built tent,
    Till the calm rivers,lakes, and seas,

Like strips of the sky fallen through me on high,
      Are each paved with the moon and these.

I bind the Sun's throne with a burning zone,
      And the Moon's with a girdle of pearl;
The volcanoes are dim, and the stars reel and swim,
      When the whirlwinds my banner unfurl.
From cape to cape, with a bridge-like shape,
      Over the torrent sea,
Sunbeam-proof, I hang like a roof, –
      The mountains its column be.
The triumphal arch through which I march
      With hurricane, fire, and snow,
When the Powers of the air are chained to my chair,
      Is the million-coloured bow;
The sphere-fire above its soft colours wove,
      While the moist Earth was laughing below.
I am the daughter of Earth and Water,
      And the nursling of the Sky;
I pass through the pores of the ocean and shores;
      I change, but I cannot die.
For after the rain when with never a stain
      The pavilion of Heaven is bare,
And the winds and sunbeams with their convex
                                    gleams
      Build up the blue dome of air,
I silently laugh at my own cenotaph,
      And out of the caverns of rain,
Like a child from the womb, like a ghost from the
                                    tomb,
      I arise and unbuild it again.

HYMN OF PAN

I

FROM THE forests and highlands
    We come, we come;
From the river-girt islands,
    Where loud waves are dumb
        Listening to my sweet pipings.
The wind in the reeds and the rushes,
    The bees on the bells of thyme,
The birds on the myrtle bushes,
    The cicadas above in the lime,
And the lizards below in the grass,
Were as silent as ever old Tmolus was,
        Listening to my sweet pipings.

II

Liquid Peneus was flowing,
    And all dark Temple lay
In Pelion's shadow, outgrowing
    The light of the dying day,
        Speeded by my sweet pipings.
The Sileni, and Sylvans, and Fauns,
    And the Nymphs of the woods and the waves,
To the edge of the moist river-lawns,
    And the brink of the dewy caves,
And all that did then attend and follow,

Were silent with love, as you now, Apollo,
    With envy of my sweet pipings.

III

I sang of the dancing stars,
    I sang of the daedal earth,
And of Heaven - and the giant wars,
    And Love, and Death, and Birth, -
        And then I changed my pipings, -
Singing how down the vale of Maenalus
    I pursued a maiden and clasped a reed,
Gods and men, we are all deluded thus!
    It breaks in our bosom and then we bleed:
All wept, as I think both ye now would,
If envy or age had not frozen your blood,
    At the sorrow of my sweet pipings.

from ORPHEUS

As I have seen
A fierce south blast tear through the darkened sky,
Driving along a rack of winged clouds,
Which may not pause, but ever hurry on,
As their wild shepherd wills them, while the stars,
Twinkling and dim, peep from between the plumes.
Anon the sky is cleared, and the high dome
Of serene heaven, starred with fiery flowers,
Shuts in the shaken earth; or the still moon
Swiftly, yet gracefully, begins her walk,
Rising all bright behind the eastern hills.
I talk of moon,a and wind, and stars, and not
Of song; but, would I echo his high song,
Nature must lend me words ne'er used before,
Or I must borrow from her perfect works,
To picture forth his perfect attributes.
He does no longer sit upon his throne
Of rock upon a desert herbless plain,
For the evergreen and knotted ilexes,
And cypresses that seldom wave their boughs,
And sea-green olives with their grateful fruit,
And elms dragging along their twisted veins,
Which drop their berries as they follow fast,
And blackthorn bushes with their infant race
Of blushing rose-blooms; beeches, to lovers dear,
And weeping willow trees; all swift or slow,
As their huge boughs or lighter dress permit,

Have circled in his throne, and Earth herself
Has sent from her maternal breast a growth
Of starlike flowers and herbs of odour sweet,
To pave the temple that his poesy
Has framed, while near his feet grim lions couch,
And kids, fearless from love, creep near his lair.
Even the blind worms seem to feel the sound.
The birds are silent, hanging down their heads,
Perched on the lowest branches of the trees;
Not even the nightingale intrudes a note
In rivalry, but all entranced she listens.

SONG

I

RARELY, RARELY, comest thou,
   Spirit of Delight!
Wherefore hast thou left me now
   Many a day and night?
Many a weary night and day
'Tis since thou art fled away.

II

How shall ever one like me
   Win thee back again?
With the joyous and the free
   Thou wilt scoff at pain.
Spirit false! thou hadst forgot
   All but those who need thee not.

III

As a lizard with the shade
   Of a trembling leaf,
Thou with sorrow art dismayed;
   Even the sighs of grief
Reproach thee, that thou art not near,

And reproach thou wilt not hear.

IV

Let me set my mournful ditty
    To a merry measure;
Thou wilt never come for pity,
    Thou wilt come for pleasure;
Pity then ill cut away
Those cruel wings, and thou wilt stay.

V

I love all that thou lovest,
    Spirit of Delight!
The fresh Earth in new leaves dressed
    And the starry night;
Autumn evening, and the morn
When the golden mists are born.

VI

I love snow,a and all the forms
    Of the radiant frost;
I love waves, and winds,a and storms,
    Everything almost
Which is Nature's, and may be
Untainted by man's misery.

VII

I love tranquil solitude,
    And such society
As is quiet, wise, and good;
    Between thee and me
What difference? but thou dost possess
The things I seek, not love them less.

VIII

I love Love – though he has wings,
    And like light can flee,
But above all other things,
    Spirit, I love thee –
Thou art love and life! Oh, come,
Make once more my heart thy home.

OZYMANDIAS

I MET a traveller from an antique land
Who said: 'Two vast and trunkless legs of stone
Stand in the desert. Near them, on the sand,
Half sunk, a shattered visage lies, whose frown,
And wrinkled lip, and sneer of cold command,
Tell that its sculptor well those passions read
Which yet survive, stamped on these lifeless things,
The hand that mocked them and the heart that fed.
And on the pedestal these words appear –
"My name is Ozymandias, king of kings:
Look on my works, ye Mighty, and despair!"
Nothing beside remains. Round the decay
Of that colossal wreck, boundless and bare
The lone and level sands stretch far away.'

SONG OF PROSPERINE

SACRED GODDESS, Mother Earth,
Thou from whose immortal bosom
Gods and men and beasts have birth,
Leaf and blade, and bud and blossom,
Breathe thine influence most divine
On thine own child, Proserpine.

If with mists of evening dew
Thou dost nourish these young flowers
Till they grow in scent and hue
Fairest children of the Hours,
Breathe thine influence most divine
On thine own child, Proserpine.

TO NIGHT

SWIFTLY WALK o'er the western wave,
Spirit of Night!
Out of the misty eastern cave,
Where, all the long and lone daylight,
Thou wovest dreams of joy and fear,
Which make thee terrible and dear –
Swift be thy flight!

Wrap thy form in a mantle gray,
Star-inwrought!
Blind with thine hair the eyes of day;
Kiss her until she be wearied out,
Then wander o'er city, and sea, and land,
Touching all with thine opiate wand –
Come, long-sought!

When I arose and saw the dawn,
I sighed for thee;
When light rode high, and the dew was gone,
And noon lay heavy on flower and tree,
And the weary day turned to his rest,
Lingering like an unloved guest,
I sighed for thee.

Thy brother Death came, and cried,
Wouldst thou me?
Thy sweet child Sleep, the filmy-eyed,

Murmured like a noontide bee,
Shall I nestle near thy side?
Wouldst thou me? – And I replied,
No, not thee!

Death will come when thou art dead,
Soon, too soon –
Sleep will come when thou art fled;
Of neither would I ask the boon
I ask of thee, beloved Night –
Swift be thine approaching flight,
Come soon, soon!

STANZAS WRITTEN IN DEJECTION
NEAR NAPLES

THE SUN is warm, the sky is clear,
The waves are dancing fast and bright,
Blue isles and snowy mountains wear
The purple noon's transparent might,
The breath of the moist earth is light,
Around its unexpanded buds;
Like many a voice of one delight
The winds, the birds, the ocean floods,
The city's voice itself, is soft like Solitude's.

I see the deep's untrampled floor
With green and purple seaweeds strown;
I see the waves upon the shore,
Like light dissolved in star-showers, thrown:
I sit upon the sands alone, –
The lightning of the noontide ocean
Is flashing round me, and a tone
Arises from its measured motion,
How sweet! did any heart now share in my emotion.

Alas! I have nor hope nor health,
Nor peace within nor calm around,
Nor that content surpassing wealth
The sage in meditation found,
And walked with inward glory crowned –
Nor fame nor power, nor love, nor leisure,

Others I see whom these surround –
Smiling they live, and call life pleasure; –
To me that cup has been dealt in another measure.

Yet now despair itself is mild,
Even as the winds and waters are;
I could lie down like a tired child,
And weep away the life of care
Which I have born and yet must bear,
Till death like sleep might steal on me,
And I might feel in the warm air
My cheek grow cold, and hear the sea
Breathe o'er my dying brain its last monotony.

Some might lament that I were cold,
As I, when this sweet day is gone,
Which my lost heart, too soon grown old,
Insults with this untimely moan;
They might lament – for I am one
Whom men love not, – and yet regret,
Unlike this day, which, when the sun
Shall on its stainless glory set,
Will linger, though enjoyed, like joy in memory yet.

MUTABILITY

WE ARE the clouds that veil the midnight moon;
How restlessly they speed, and gleam, and quiver,
Streaking the darkness radiantly! – yet soon
Night closes round, and they are lost forever:

Or like forgotten lyres, whose dissonant strings
Give various response to each varying blast,
To whose frail frame no second motion brings
One mood or modulation like the last.

We rest. – A dream has power to poison sleep;
We rise. – One wandering thought pollutes the day;
We feel, conceive or reason, laugh or weep;
Embrace fond foe, or cast our cares away:

It is the same! – For, be it joy or sorrow,
The path of its departure still is free:
Man's yesterday may ne'er be like his morrow;
Nought may endure but Mutability.

A SUMMER EVENING CHURCHYARD, LECHDALE, GLOUCESTERSHIRE

THE WIND has swept from the wide atmosphere
Each vapour that obscured the sunset's ray,
And pallid Evening twines its beaming hair
In duskier braids around the languid eyes of Day:
Silence and Twilight, unbeloved of men,
Creep hand in hand from yon obscurest glen.

They breathe their spells towards the departing day,
Encompassing the earth, air, stars, and sea;
Light, sound, and motion, own the potent sway,
Responding to the charm with its own mystery.
The winds are still, or the dry church-tower grass
Knows not their gentle motions as they pass.

Thou too, aerial pile, whose pinnacles
Point from one shrine like pyramids of fire,
Obey'st I in silence their sweet solemn spells,
Clothing in hues of heaven thy dim and distant spire,
Around whose lessening and invisible height
Gather among the stars the clouds of night.

The dead are sleeping in their sepulchres:
And, mouldering as they sleep, a thrilling sound,
Half sense half thought, among the darkness stirs,
Breathed from their wormy beds all living things

　　　　　　　　　　　　　　　around,
And, mingling with the still night and mute sky,
Its awful hush is felt inaudibly.

Thus solemnized and softened, death is mild
And terrorless as this serenest night.
Here could I hope, like some enquiring child
Sporting on graves, that death did hide from human
　　　　　　　　　　　　　　　　　　sight
Sweet secrets, or beside its breathless sleep
That loveliest dreams perpetual watch did keep.

AUTUMN: A DIRGE

THE WARM sun is falling, the bleak wind is wailing,
The bare boughs are sighing, the pale flowers are
                                                  dying,
And the Year
On the earth is her death-bed, in a shroud of leaves
                                                  dead,
Is lying.
Come, Months, come away,
From November to May,
In your saddest array;
Follow the bier
Of the dead cold Year,
And like dim shadows watch by her sepulchre.

The chill rain is falling, the nipped worm is
                                                  crawling,
The rivers are swelling, the thunder is knelling
For the Year;
The blithe swallows are flown, and the lizards each
                                                  gone
To his dwelling.
Come, Months, come away;
Put on white, black and gray;
Let your light sisters play –
Ye, follow the bier
Of the dead cold Year,
And make her grave green with tear on tear.

TO WORDSWORTH

POET OF Nature, thou hast wept to know
That things depart which never may return:
Childhood and youth, friendship and love's first glow,
Have fled like sweet dreams, leaving thee to mourn.
These common woes I feel. One loss is mine
Which thou too feel'st, yet I alone deplore.
Thou wert as a lone star, whose light did shine
On some frail bark in winter's midnight roar:
Thou hast like to a rock-built refuge stood
Above the blind and battling multitude:
In honoured poverty thy voice did weave
Songs consecrate to truth and liberty, –
Deserting these, thou leavest me to grieve,
Thus having been, that thou shouldst cease to be.
***

LINES

1

THE COLD earth slept below,
　Above the cold sky shone;
　　And all around, with a chilling sound,
　　From caves of ice and fields of snow,
The breath of night like death did flow
　　Beneath the sinking moon.

2

The wintry hedge was black,
　The green grass was not seen,
　　The birds did rest on the bare thorn's breast,
　　Whose roots, beside the pathway track,
Had bound their folds o'er many a crack
　　Which the frost had made between.

3

Thine eyes glowed in the glare
　Of the moon's dying light;
　　As a fen-fire's beam on a sluggish stream
　　Gleams dimly, so the moon shone there,
And it yellowed the strings of thy raven hair,
　　That shook in the wind of night.

4

The moon made thy lips pale, beloved –
    The wind made thy bosom chill –
        The night did shed on thy dear head
        Its frozen dew, and thou didst lie
Where the bitter breath of the naked sky
        Might visit thee at will.

LINES

1

THAT TIME is dead for ever, child!
Drowned, frozen, dead for ever!
We look on the past
And stare aghast
At the spectres wailing, pale and ghast,
Of hopes which thou and I beguiled
To death on life's dark river.

2

The stream we gazed on then rolled by;
Its waves are unreturning;
But we yet stand
In a lone land,
Like tombs to mark the memory
Of hopes and fears, which fade and flee
In the light of life's dim morning.

'O THAT A CHARIOT OF CLOUD WERE MINE'

O THAT a chariot of cloud were mine!
Of cloud which the wild tempest weaves in air,
When the moon over the ocean's line
Is spreading the locks of her bright gray hair.
O that a chariot of cloud were mine!
I would sail on the waves of the billowy wind
To the mountain peak and the rocky lake,
And the...

THE PAST

1

WILT THOU forget the happy hours
Which we buried in Love's sweet bowers,
Heaping over their corpses cold
Blossoms and leaves, instead of mould?
Blossoms which were the joys that fell,
And leaves, the hopes that yet remain.

2

Forget the dead, the past? Oh, yet
There are ghosts that may take revenge for it,
Memories that make the heart a tomb,
Regrets which glide through the spirit's gloom,
And with ghastly whispers tell
That joy, once lost, is pain.

TO MARY —

O MARY DEAR, that you were here
With your brown eyes bright and clear.
And your sweet voice, like a bird
Singing love to its lone mate
In the ivy bower disconsolate;
Voice the sweetest ever heard!
And your brow more…
Than the … sky
Of this azure Italy.
Mary dear, come to me soon,
I am not well whilst thou art far;
As sunset to the sphered moon,
As twilight to the western star,
Thou, beloved, art to me.

O Mary dear, that you were here;
The Castle echo whispers 'Here!'

AN EXHORTATION

CHAMELEONS FEED on light and air:
   Poets' food is love and fame:
If in this wide world of care
   Poets could but find the same
With as little toil as they,
   Would they ever change their hue
   As the light chameleons do,
     Suiting it to every ray
     Twenty times a day?

Poets are on this cold earth,
   As chameleons might be,
Hidden from their early birth
   In a cave beneath the sea;
Where light is, chameleons change:
   Where love is not, poets do:
   Fame is love disguised: if few
     Find either, never think it strange
     That poets range.

Yet dare not stain with wealth or power
   A poet's free and heavenly mind:
If bright chameleons should devour
   Any food but beams and wind,
They would grow as earthly soon
   As their brother lizards are.
   Children of a sunnier star,

Spirits from beyond the moon,
Oh, refuse the boon!

THE BIRTH OF PLEASURE

AT THE creation of the Earth
Pleasure, that divinest birth,
From the soil of Heaven did rise,
Wrapped in sweet wild melodies –
Like an exhalation wreathing
To the sound of air low-breathing
Through Aeolian pines, which make
A shade and shelter to the lake
Whence it rises soft and slow;
Her life-breathing [limbs] did flow
In the harmony divine
Of an ever-lengthening line
Which enwrapped her perfect form
With a beauty clear and warm.

SONNET

YE HASTEN to the grave! What seek ye there,
Ye restless thoughts and busy purposes
Of the idle brain, which the world's livery wear?
O thou quick heart, which pantest to possess
All that pale Expectation feigneth fair!
Thou vainly curious mind which wouldest guess
Whence thou didst come, and whither thou must go,
And all that never yet was known would know –
Oh, whither hasten ye, that thus ye press,
With such swift feet life's green and pleasant path,
Seeking, alike from happiness and woe,
A refuge in the cavern of gray death?
O heart, and mind, and thoughts! what thing do you
Hope to inherit in the grave below?

HYMN OF APOLLO

I

THE SLEEPLESS Hours who watch me as I lie,
   Curtained with star-inwoven tapestries
From the broad moonlight of the sky,
   Fanning the busy dreams from my dim eyes, –
Waken me when their Mother, the gray Dawn,
Tells them that dreams and that the moon is gone.

II

Then I arise, and climbing heaven's blue dome,
   I walk over the mountains and the waves,
Leaving my robe upon the ocean foam;
   My footsteps pave the clouds with fire; the caves
Are filled with my bright presence, and the air
Leaves the green Earth to my embraces bare.

III

The sunbeams are my shafts, with which I kill
   Deceit, that loves the night and fears the day;
All men who do or even imagine ill
   Fly me, and from the glory of my ray

Good minds and open actions take new might,
Until diminished by the reign of Night.

IV

I feed the clouds, the rainbows and the flowers
    With their aethereal colours; the moon's globe
And the pure stars in their eternal bowers
    Are cinctured with my power as with a robe;
Whatever lamps on Earth or heaven may shine
Are portions of one power, which is mine.

V

I stand at noon upon the peak of Heaven,
    Then with unwilling steps I wander down
Into the clouds of the Atlantic even;
    For grief that I depart they weep and frown:
What look is more delightful than the smile
With which I soothe them from the western isle?

VI

I am the eye with which the Universe
    Beholds itself and knows itself divine;
All harmony of instrument or verse,
    All prophecy, all medicine is mine,
All light of art or nature; – to my song
Victory and praise in its own right belong.

from EPIPSYCHIDION

SERAPH OF Heaven! too gentle to be human,
Veiling beneath that radiant form of Woman
All that is insupportable in thee
Of light, and love, and immortality!
Sweet benediction in the eternal Curse!
Veiled Glory of this lampless Universe!
Thou Moon beyond the clouds! Thou living Form
Among the Dead! Thou Star above the Storm!
Thou Wonder, and thou beauty, and thou Terror!
Thou Harmony of Nature's art! Thou Mirror
In whom, as in the splendour of the sun,
All shapes look glorious which thou gazest on!
Ay, even the dim words which obscure thee now
Flash, lightning-like, with unaccustomed glow;
I pray thee that thou blot from this sad song
All of its much mortality and wrong,
With those clear drops, which start like sacred dew
From the twin lights thy sweet soul darkens through,
Weeping, till sorrow becomes ecstasy:
Then smile on it, so that it may not die.

•

Twin Spheres of light who rule this passive Earth,
This world of love, this *me*; and into birth
Awaken all its fruits and flowers, and dart
Magnetic might into its central heart;

And lift its billows and its mists, and guide
By everlasting laws, each wind and tide
To its fit cloud, and its appointed cave;
And lull its storms, each in the craggy grave
Which was its cradle, luring to faint bowers
The armies of the rainbow-wingèd showers;
And, as those married lights, which from the towers
Of heaven look forth and fold the wandering globe
In liquid sleep and splendour, as a robe;
And all their many-mingled influence blend,
If equal, yet unlike, to one sweet end;-
So ye, bright regents, with alternate sway
Govern my sphere of being, night and day!
Thou, not disdaining even a borrowed might;
Thou, not eclipsing a remoter light;
And, through the shadow of the seasons three,
From Spring to autumn's sere maturity,
Light it into the Winter of the tomb,
Where it may ripen to a brighter bloom.
Thou too, O Comet beautiful and fierce,
Who drew the heart of this frail Universe
Towards thine own; till, wrecked in that convulsion,
Alternating attraction and repulsion,
Thine went astray and that was rent in twain;
Of, float into our azure heaven again!

•

                              Meanwhile
We two will rise, and sit, and walk together,
Under the roof of blue Ionian weather,
And wander in the meadows, or ascend
The mossy mountains, where the blue heavens bend

With lightest winds, to touch their paramour;
Or linger, where the pebble-paven shore,
Under the quick, faint kisses of the sea
Possessing and possessed by all that is
Within that calm circumference of bliss,
And by each other, till to love and live
Be one: – or, at the noontide hour, arrive
Where some old cavern hoar seems yet to keep
The moonlight of the expired night asleep,
Through which the awakened day can never peep;
A Veil for our seclusion, close as night's,
Where secure sleep may kill thine innocent lights;
Sleep, the fresh dew of languid love, the rain
Whose drops quench kisses till they burn again.
And we will talk, until thought's melody
Become too sweet for utterance, and it die
In words, to live again in looks, which dart
With thrilling tone into the voiceless heart,
Harmonizing silence without a sound.
Our breathing shall intermix, our bosoms bound,
And our veins beat together; and our lips
With other eloquence than words, eclipse
The soul that burns between them, and the wells
Which boil under our being's inmost cells,
The fountains of our deepest life, shall be
Confused in Passion's golden purity,
As mountain-springs under the morning sun.
We shall become the same,we shall be one
Spirit within two frames, oh! wherefore two?
One passion in twin-hearts, which grows and grew,
Till like two meteors of expanding flame.
Those spheres instinct with it become the same,
Touch, mingle, are transfigured; ever still

Burning, yet ever inconsumable:
In one another's substance finding food,
Like flames too pure and light and unimbued
To nourish their bright lives with baser prey,
Which point to heaven and cannot pass away:
One hope within two wills, one will beneath
Two overshadowing minds, one life, one death,
One heaven, one Hell, one immortality,
And one annihilation. Woe is me!
The wingèd words on which my soul would pierce
Into the height of Love's rare Universe,
Are chains of lead around its flight of fire –
I pant, I sink, I tremble, I expire!

ILLUSTRATIONS

Percy Bysshe Shelley

Alfred Clint, Percy Shelley, 1819

Edward Onslow Ford, Shelley Memorial, Oxford

Richard Rothwell, Portrait of Mary Shelley, 1840

Joseph Severn, Percy Shelley, 1845

Percy Shelley, Mary Shelley and Lord Byron
in The Bride of Frankenstein (1935)

Gothic (Ken Russell, 1986),
with Julian Sands as Shelley

A NOTE ON
PERCY BYSSHE SHELLEY

But poetry acts in another and diviner manner. It awakens and enlarges the mind itself by rendering it the receptacle of a thousand unapprehended combinations of thought. Poetry lifts the veil from the hidden beauty of the world and makes familiar objects be as if they were not familiar; it re-produces all that it represents, and the impersonations clothed in its Elysian light stand thenceforward in the minds of those who have once contemplated them as memorials of that gentle and exalted content with extends itself over all thoughts and actions with which it coexists.

Percy Bysshe Shelley, *A Defence of Poetry*[1]

PERCY BYSSHE SHELLEY IS one of the 'major' British poets, seen by many, still, as the breathless, hyperlyrical, angelic yet anarchic poet of the Romantic era, out-doing Byron and Keats in terms of sheer brilliance. His personality, as with Keats and Byron, is a crucial component in the Shelley cult. For Shelley has a cult built up around him, like, say, van Gogh, Leonardo or Jackson Pollock among painters; Beethoven, Mozart and Wagner among composers; Valentino, Brando and Monroe among movie stars. Shelley's life, so much more colourful than, say, Thomas Hardy's or Philip Larkin's life, is a crucial element in the raising up of him as a 'great' British poet. Sad but true. Roguish, adventurous, decadent lives help to sell

---

[1] Shelley: *A Defence of Poetry*, quoted in *Selected Poetry and Prose*, 212

art, no question. Look at Arthur Rimbaud, or D. H. Lawrence.

When you look at Shelley's poetry, trying to ignore or forget the personality cult, you see flashes of magnificence, moments of sublime word magic, but also tedium and banality. The problem is, partly, that Shelley overwrites. He can produce short, powerful poems (such as 'To a Skylark', 'A Lament', and 'Song of Prosperine'). But, much more typical is the long or even 'epic' poem, such as *The Revolt of Islam, Queen Mab, Adonais* and, probably his best work, taken as a whole, *Prometheus Unbound.* Shelley's propensity for extended lyrical sequences makes him, on a mundane level, difficult to anthologize or edit. More importantly, it means that his poetic power can all too often become diffused over too many stanzas.

True, it takes time for Shelley to work up his poetic magic. But just as frequently, it seems, the poetic magic simply does not come. Or it is dissolved, runs thin, like paint without pigment.

Another common criticism of Shelley is that he is simply too achingly 'pure', too blissfully Platonic and idealistic. Instead of real things, critics argue, Shelley gives us effects and idealism. Hazlitt wrote:

> He gives us, for representations of things, rhapsodies of words. He does not lend the colours of the imagination and the ornaments of style to the objects of nature, but paints gaudy, flimsy, allegorical pictures on gauze, on the cobwebs of his own brain.[2]

F. R. Leavis criticized Shelley for his 'weak grasp on the actual', while W. H. Auden found him also weak in the area of direct experience. C. S. Lewis wrote: '[i]n his metre, with all it sweetness, there is much ignoble fluidity, much of mere jingle.'[3] Leavis laid into Shelley's luxurious poesie, his luxury in the poignancy' as he called it.[4] Shelley's greatness could all too soon

---

2 Hazlitt: *On People of Sense*, quoted in Hodgart, 113

3 C. S. Lewis: *Rehabilitation and Other Essays*, Oxford University Press 1939

4 F. R. Leavis: *Revaluation: Tradition and Development in English Poetry*, Chatto & Windus 1949, and in M. H. Abrams, ed: *English Romantic Poets: Modern Essays in Criticism*, Oxford University Press, New York 1975, 356

become his weakness, Leavis claimed.[5] Leavis could not abide Shelley's vagueness, the seeming incoherence of his poetic language:

> We have them in their most innocent aspect in those favourite words: *radiant, aëral, odorous, daedal, faint, sweet, bright, winged, - inwoven*, and the rest of the fondled vocabulary that any reader of Shelley could go on enumerating. They manifest themselves as decidedly deplorable in *The Cloud* and *To a Skylark*, which illustrate the dangers of fostering the kind of inspiration that works only when critical intelligence is switched off.[6]

Yet, funnily enough, precisely the same criticisms could be brought against the author Leavis championed so energetically, D. H. Lawrence, who had his own extremely ambivalent and vague 'fondled vocabulary', consisting of words such as *loins, darkness, strange* and *fecund*. Leavis has not bothered to read Shelley's favourite words in context of his poetry, as he does with Lawrence. Both Lawrence and Shelley are poets of the body and Nature, of sensations and experiences, and they have their own 'fondled vocabulary' to (try to) describe such sensations. Leavis objects to Shelley's *radiant, faint, sweet* and *winged*, while adoring Lawrence's equally vague *strange, darkness, loins* and *fecund*.

Leavis quoted from one of Shelley's most famous poetic moments:

> Thou on whose stream, mid the steep sky's commotion,
> Loose clouds like earth's decaying leaves are shed,
> Shook from the tangled boughs of Heaven and Ocean,
>
> Angels of rain and lightning: there are spread
> On the blue surface of thine aëry surge,
> Like the bright hair uplifted from the head
>
> Of some fierce Maenad, even from the dim verge
> Of the horizon to the zenith's height,
> The locks of the approaching storm.

Leavis comments on this extract thus:[7]

---

5 'The poetry in which Shelley's genius manifests itself characteristically and for which he has his place in the English tradition, is much more closely related to his weaknesses.' Leavis, in Abrams, 362

6 Leavis, in Abrams, 352

7 Leavis, op. Cit., 346

∗ *93*

The sweeping movement of the verse, with the accompanying plangency, is so potent that, as many can testify, it is possible to have been for years familiar with the Ode - to know it by heart - without asking the obvious questions. In what respects are the 'loose clouds' like 'decaying leaves'? The correspondence is certainly not in shape, colour or way of moving. Or it is only the vague general sense of windy tumult that associates the clouds and the leaves; and, accordingly, the appropriateness of the metaphor 'stream' in the first line is not that it suggests a surface on which, leaves, the clouds might be 'shed,' but that it contributes to the general 'streaming' effect in which the inappropriateness of 'shed' passes unnoticed. What again, are those 'tangled boughs of Heaven and Ocean'? They stand for nothing that Shelley could have pointed to in the scene before him, the 'boughs,' it is plain, have grown out of the 'leaves' in the previous line, and we are not to ask what the tree is.

True, Shelley is supremely idealistic, full of idealism. His philosophy of life takes much from Plato, and from later Neoplatonism.

Plato, of course, often found it difficult to reconcile the manifestations of Nature with the essences and beauties of Idealism. In Shelley, as in so much of Romantic poetry, Nature is idealized and idealism is treated in a naturalistic fashion. For the poet, there is not necessarily a conflict between ideas and actualities, between dreams and waking experiences, or or or between art and life. In poems such as 'The Cloud', 'Ode to the West Wind' and 'To a Skylark', Shelley demonstrates a delicate and detailed grasp of meteorology,and the poetry of weather. When it comes to nature poetry and nature mysticism, Shelley turns out to be as successful as that god of English pantheism, Wordsworth. Throughout Shelley's poetry the force of Nature rages. At times, all he does is to conjure up scenes, or to list effects and visions, just like Keats in 'The Eve of St Agnes' or Wordsworth in *The Prelude*. Nature poetry can read as a series of linguistic fireworks, without much substance. You can see Henry Vaughan, Shakespeare, Novalis, Goethe and Wordsworth as producers of lists of natural effects. Taken out of the context of the lengthy pieces such as *Prometheus Unbound, The Revolt of Islam* or *Queen Mab*, Shelley's' nature poetry bears up well to detailed analysis, as well as consumption simply for entertainment. 'Poetry is ever accompanied with pleasure' Shelley writes in *A Defence of Poetry*.[8]

Art must entertain as well enrich or enlighten, and Shelley, like Keats or

---

8 Shelley: *Selected Poetry and Prose*, 210

Heine, is certainly entertaining. He is full of exuberantly described images of rivers, forests, suns, cities, maenads and deities. Shelley might be over-lush for some tastes. Certainly he is as rich a poet, in terms of sensual imagery, as there is. Certainly, too, he is in love with his ability to create word-pictures. He is self-conscious about his word magic. He knows what he is doing with his poetic effects. Trouble is, he can't stop himself using them. He seems unable to stop himself from gushing. He does gush, sumptuously, lusciously, deliciously. At times Shelley is all too delicate, all too self-consciously elegant. Many of his lines end, like those of Goethe or Keats, with an exclamation mark. He writes, so often, in a state of great excitement: 'clasped my hands in ecstasy!' ('Hymn to Intellectual Beauty'), '[p]aradise of golden lights!' ('Ode to Heaven'), '[v]oice the sweetest ever heard!' ('To Mary ---'), 'thou shouldst now depart!' ('Adonais').

This is typical Shelley, this outpouring of poesie lit up with exclamation marks like so many candles. Shelley's poetry does not burn fervently, like Keats' or Rimbaud's; rather, it shines or scintillates fervently, like Dante's. There is a radiance - of summer, of sunlight, of the beloved's eyes, of various gods - at the heart of Shelley's work. In his *Queen Mab* he writes of 'the sun's broad orb', 'purple gold', 'intolerable radiancy', 'far clouds of feathery gold', 'golden islands/ Gleaming in yon flood light', 'the sun's bright couch', 'floors of flashing light' - and this in just two stanzas.[9] Shelley seems to want to outdo Dante in the creation of a luminous world called Heaven.

You can see this fundamental, Gnostic Light throughout Shelley's art: in 'Adonais' ('[t]hat Light whose smile kindles the Universe'). Dante freighted his *Divina Commedia* with a dazzling light, which was Love or God. In Shelley, too we find the same idealization of light, as Light, or Love, or God, or Apollo. Dante's Neoplatonic but thoroughly mediaeval and Christian poetic construction becomes in Shelley a post-Renaissance and quasi-pagan/ Hellenic edifice. But it is the eternal light, whether this light is Love or God, that Shelley celebrates in so many poems. In his last poem, 'The Triumph of Life', he writes:

---

9 Shelley: *Poetical Works*, ed Thomas Hutchinson, Oxford University Press 1905/43, 766-7

'And, as I looked, the bright omnipresence
Of morning through the orient cavern flowed,
And the sun's image radiantly intense

'Burned on the waters of the well that glowed
Like gold, and threaded all the forest's maze
With winding paths of emerald fire; there stood

'Amid the sun, as he amid the blaze
Of his own glory, on the vibrating
Floor of the fountain, paved with flashing rays,

'A Shape all light, which with one hand did fling
Dew on the earth, as if she were the dawn...'[10]

'The Triumph of Life' displays Shelley piling on one vision or effect after another. In Shelley, as in Keats or Dante, there is always *one more thing* that will astonish the reader. The poet sets before us the riches of his narrative, but, no matter how wondrous it is, there is always *more* to come. This is the banquet that Romantic poetry provides: not just plenty to eat, but more than plenty, and then some more. Poetry, *and then some*, as American vernacular has it. With Eichendorff, Hugo, Wordsworth and other Romantics, we always seem to get poetry *and then some*.

For Catherine Belsey, Shelley's poetry is typical of Romantic poetry, because it is, ultimately, about its own making, rather than 'about' clouds or gods or love or emotions. It is a poetry that is a sophisticated mirror. Belsey writes:

In the Romantic ode poetry enshrines the record of its own birth. The account of the vision is the poem itself and therefore it is the poem which constitutes the proof of the validity of the vision, the truth of the intimations of immortality which the text records. The poem then generates in the reader a participation in these intimations, and this is the source of its power to transcend and transform the world, to redeem it from death. In Shelley's version the West Wind symbolizes both the poetic vision which is to bring life to the poet and the 'incantation' of the poem itself which will 'quicken a new birth' in the dying world. The poem is thus a perfect circle, autonomous and self-contained, emblem and evidence of its own values, immortalizing the ephemeral vision and so offering the gift of life to its readers.[11]

---

10 in *Poetical Works*, 515

11 Catherine Belsey: *Critical Practice,*

For Shelley, as for so many other Romantic poets, poetry expands life, it renews and replenishes life. In *A Defence of Poetry* Shelley writes: '[p]oetry enlarges the circumference of the imagination by replenishing it with thoughts of ever new delight, which have the power of attracting and assimilating to their own nature all other thoughts, and which form new intervals and interstices whose void forever craves fresh food.'[12] For Shelley, as for Keats, Goethe, Novalis and other Romantic poets, the poet is something of a shaman, a magician who conjure up astonishing experiences. As Shelley says in the extract quoted above from *A Defence of Poetry*, Shelley writes that '[p]oetry lifts the veil from the hidden beauty of the world and makes familiar objects be as if they were not familiar...' For Shelley, poetry enlarges experience of the world, so that things come alive. For him, poets are shamans, not prophets, but magicians. 'A poet participates in the eternal, the infinite, and the one' says Shelley.[13] Shelley's poet creates also for companionship, singing like a nightingale in darkness. 'A poet is a nightingale, who sits in darkness and sings to cheer its own solitude with sweet sounds'.[14] Shelley's huge outpourings can be seen as a mirror, a vast form of companionship, much in the manner as Samuel Beckett's protagonist in *Company* speaks for 'company',

Shelley loves to dazzle. In *Prometheus Unbound* we have those big set pieces, staged with the panoply of gods and goddesses – Jupiter, Juno, Demogorgon, Moon, Earth, Asia, Chorus of Spirits and Prometheus. The result is highly theatrical, self-consciously showy, reminiscent of the masque that Prospero curtails so abruptly in *The Tempest*. Of course, *The Tempest*, with its magus and wind-blown sprites, its evocation of paganism, Hellenism and magic, its vivacious sense of 'anarchy', is the Shakespeare play most appropriate for Shelley's poetic world.

Shelley's poetry is very erotic. That is obvious from the yearning or Platonic vision of a *unio mystica* at the end of *Epipsychidion* where Shelley hits all the right Gnostic-Neoplatonic notes, speaking of souls burning like flames, of 'Passion's golden purity', of breath intermixing, of two hearts becoming one. This is the gnostic/ Platonic dream at the heart

---

12 Shelley, *Selected Poetry and Prose*, 212
13 Shelley, *Selected Poetry and Prose*, 207
14 Shelley, in ib., 211

of Western eroticism, this idea of the total fusion of two souls in love, which lies behind Bronte's *Wuthering Heights,* Hardy's *Tess of the d'Urbervilles,* Dante's *Vita Nuova,* Petrarch's *Canzoniere,* Shakespeare's sonnets, Sceve's *Delie* and Lawrence's *The Rainbow.* But Shelley's poetic eroticism is apparent from all his poetry: it infuses his style, his descriptions, his tone, his choice of words, and, of course, his subject matter, imagery, his themes. The sexuality of Shelley's work is apparent too in his prose, in his descriptions of poetry, his aesthetics and metaphysics. In the Preface to *The Revolt of Islam,* he writes in a bombastic, phallic manner of his adventures:

> I aspire to be something better. The circumstance of my accidental education have been favourable to this ambition. I have been familiar from boyhood with mountains and lakes and the sea, and the solitude of forests: Danger, which sports upon the brink of precipices, has been my playmate. I have trodden the glaciers of the Alps, and lived under the eye of Mont Blanc. I have been a wanderer among distant fields. I have sailed down mighty rivers, and seen the sun rise and set, and the stars come forth, whilst I have sailed night and day down a rapid stream among mountains.. I have seen populous cities, and have watched the passions which rise and spread, and sink and change, amongst assembled multitudes of men. I have seen the theatre of the more visible ravages of tyranny and war; cities and villages reduced to scattered groups of black and roofless houses,and the naked inhabitants sitting famished upon their desolated thresholds. I have conversed with men of genius. The poetry of ancient Greece and Rome, and modern Italy, and our own country, has been to me, like external nature, a passion and an enjoyment.

Like the 'real life' Shelley, Shelley the poet tours the world, sweeping over it like his 'wild West wind'. The persona Shelley takes on in his poetry is of a dazzling spirit, zooming over the world, back into the past, into Greek and Roman mythology, gathering up strains of paganism, Neoplatonism, geography, philosophy, politics and history. He picks it all up as he wishes, and mixes it together, sometimes forcefully, sometimes it ends up as a syncretic mess.

In Shelley, the 'pleasure of the text' is strained to the maximum. His is the rhetoric of orgasmic bliss, as Nathaniel Brown writes: '[s]uch rhetoric, with its associative world clusters - "sinking," "perishing," "expiring," "dying," - is often consciously employed by Shelley in a sexual sense as the verbal equivalent of orgasmic annihilation.'[15] Shelley's sexuality as expressed in his works is often discussed by critics, but the man himself was far from an androgynous sylph.[16] As Brown writes: '[n]o bodiless angel, he joyously celebrated the pleasures of the senses. A knowledge of the sexual element in his work is thus indispensable to interpreting his significance.' (Brown, 2) Shelley's views or on love are essentially Platonic, shot through with immense sensuality. It is an orgasmic kind of Platonism, where sexuality and mysticism merge, as in John Cowper Powys or André Gide. The poem 'Invocation to Misery' is typical, full of erotic desire coupled with sensual awareness, and fear: '[k]iss me' the poet gasps, 'oh! thy lips are cold:/ Round my neck thine arms enfold -/ They are soft, but chill and dead'.[17] The poem, like all of Shelley's work, is based on the age old union in patriarchal metaphysics of sex and death, where bodies burn with fevers alternately hot with life and cold with death, as in Petrarch's *Rime Sparse*. Shelley produces yet another love-and-death lyric, where a kiss is the *mors osculis* or 'kiss of death' of occultism. In Shelley's vivid metaphor, there is a grave under the bridal bed. The couple copulate in an orgasm of death, with the language clear in its love-in-death thrust: the language is of 'darkness', 'oblivion', 'dread' and 'graves'. The poem exalts the cult of sex and death at the heart of Western philosophy, embodied here - as in Georges Bataille, Sigmund Freud, Wilhelm Reich, William Burroughs, André Breton, Hans Bellmer, Norman Mailer, Henry Miller, Jean-Paul Sartre, etc - by an orgasmic death:

Hasten to the bridal bed -
Underneath the grave 'tis spread:
In darkness may our love be hid,
Oblivion be our coverlid -
We may rest, and none forbid.

Clasp me till our hearts be grown

---

15 Nathaniel Brown: 130

16 Brown writes: '[e]xcept for his translation of the *Symposium* (189D-190B), Shelley nowhere uses the term *Androgyny*. Nevertheless, the idea is implicit throughout his work, particularly in his portrayal of the sexes, with their harmonious blending of the traditionally masculine and the traditionally feminine.' (215)

17 Shelley, in *Poetical Works*, 560

Like two shadows into one;
Till this dreadful transport may
Like a vapour fade away,
in the sleep that last alway.[18]

In his essay on love, Shelley wrote:

We are born into the world, and there is something within us which, from the instant that we love, more and more thirsts after its likeness...Not only the portrait of our external being, but an assemblage of the minutest particles of which our nature is composed; a mirror whose or surface reflects only the forms of purity and brightness; a soul within our soul that describes a circle around its proper Paradise which pain and sorrow and evil dare not overleap. To this we eagerly refer all sensations, thirsting that they should resemble or correspond with it.[19]

This is a classic masculine/ patriarchal view of sexuality: it is dominated by desire - feminists would say lust - for that 'mirror image' of the male, the Jungian *anima* figure, Dante's Beatrice, Tristan's Isolde, Petrarch's Laura, Antony's Cleopatra. All familiar stuff this, this masculine lust for the mirror. For feminists, it merely speaks of the vanity of the male, where men wish to see themselves and their desires reflected. The Platonic 'other half' or 'soul mate' becomes, in the patriarchal mythopoeia, a sex object, the 'obscure object of desire', as Lacanians call it, 'obscure' because always unreachable, finally. We see this clearly in Shelley, who, like Keats or Goethe, is drive by pure desire, a yearning which no amount of poetry can assuage. Shelley the poet keeps on yearning, like Ursula in Lawrence's *The Rainbow*, and knows, though he seldom admits it, that such erotic lust can *never* be satisfied. 'I can't get me no satisfaction' crooned Mick Jagger. The Rolling Stones' pop song is essentially another version of the secular lovesong, current in Western culture from Sappho through courtly love poetry and Shakespeare to the present day.

---

[18] Shelley, *Poetic Works*, 560
[19] Shelley, in *Selected Prose*, 191

Bibliography

M.H. Abrams, ed: *English Romantic Poets: Modern Essays in Criticism*, Oxford University Press, New York 1975

W. Jackson Bate: *John Keats*, Chatto & Windus 1979

Catherine Belsey: *Critical Practice*, Routledge 1980

Robert Gittings: *John Keats*, Heinemann 1968

Grahamn Hough: *The Last Romantics*, Methuen 1961

John Keats: *Poems*, ed J.E. Morpurgo, Penguin 1953

—*The Letters of John Keats*, ed Hyder Rollins, 2 vols 1958

—*Selected Poems and Letters*, ed Robert Gittings, Heinemann 1966

—*The Poetical Works of John Keats*, ed H.W. Garrod, Oxford University Press 1958

F.R. Leavis: *Revaluation: Tradition and Development in English Poetry*, Chatto & Windus 1949

C.S. Lewis: *Rehabilitation and Other Essays,* Oxford University Press 1939

Shelley: *Selected Poetry and Prose,*

—*Poetic Works*, ed ed Thomas Hutchinson, Oxford University Press, 1905/ 43

Helen Vendler: *The Odes of John Keats*, Harvard University Press, Cambridge, Mass., 1983

Ailen Ward: *John Keats: The Making of a Poet*, Secker & Warburg 1963

Beauties, Beasts, and Enchantment

CLASSIC FRENCH FAIRY TALES

Translated and with an Introduction
by Jack Zipes

A collection of 36 classic French fairy tales translated by renowned writer Jack Zipes.
Cinderella, Beauty and the Beast, Sleeping Beauty and *Little Red Riding Hood* are among the
classic fairy tales in this amazing book.
Includes illustrations from fairy tale collections.
Jack Zipes has written and published widely on fairy tales.

'Terrific... a succulent array of 17th and 18th century 'salon' fairy tales'
- *The New York Times Book Review*

'These tales are adventurous, thrilling in a way fairy tales are meant to be... The translation
from the French is modern, happily free of archaic and hyperbolic language... a fine and
sophisticated collection' - *New York Tribune*

'Enjoyable to read... a unique collection of French regional folklore' - *Library Journal*

'Charming stories accompanied by attractive pen-and-ink drawings' - *Chattanooga Times*

Introduction and illustrations   612pp.   ISBN 9781861712510 Pbk   ISBN 9781861713193 Hbk

Life, Life
Selected Poems

Arseny Tarkovsky

translated and edited by Virginia Rounding

Arseny Tarkovsky is the neglected Russian poet, father of the acclaimed film director
Andrei Tarkovsky. This new book gathers together many of Tarkovsky's most lyrical
and heartfelt poems, in Rounding's clear, new translations. Many of Tarkovsky's poems
appeared in his son's films, such as *Mirror, Stalker, Nostalghia and The Sacrifice*.
There is an introduction by Rounding, and a bibliography of both Arseny and
Andrei Tarkovsky.

Bibliography and notes 124pp 3rd ed   ISBN 9781861712660 Hbk   ISBN 9781861711144

In the Dim Void

Samuel Beckett's Late Trilogy:
Company, Ill Seen, Ill Said and Worstward Ho

by Gregory Johns

This book discusses the luminous beauty and dense, rigorous poetry of Samuel Beckett's late works, *Company, Ill Seen, Ill Said* and *Worstward Ho*. Gregory Johns looks back over Beckett's long writing career, charting the development from the *Molloy-Malone Dies-Unnamable* trilogy through the 'fizzles' of the 1960s to the elegiac lyricism of the *Company* series. Johns compares the trilogy with late plays such as *Ghosts*, *Footfalls* and *Rockaby*.

Bibliography, notes. Illustrated. 120pp
ISBN 9781861712974 Pbk and ISBN 9781861712608 Hbk
9781861713407 E-book

Thomas A. Christie

JOHN HUGHES
& EIGHTIES CINEMA
Teenage Hopes & American Dreams

John Hughes (1950-2009) is one of the best-loved figures in 1980s American filmmaking, and considered by many to be among the finest and most celebrated comedy writers of his generation. His memorable motion pictures are insightful, humanistic, culturally aware, and paint a vibrant picture of the United States in a decade of rapid social and political change.

Bibliography, notes, illustrations   372pp.
ISBN 9781861713896 Pbk   ISBN 9781861713988 Hbk
Also available: *Ferris Bueller's Day Off: Pocket Movie Guide*

CRESCENT MOON PUBLISHING

web: www.crmoon.com e-mail: cresmopub@yahoo.co.uk

ARTS, PAINTING, SCULPTURE

The Art of Andy Goldsworthy
Andy Goldsworthy: Touching Nature
Andy Goldsworthy in Close-Up
Andy Goldsworthy: Pocket Guide
Andy Goldsworthy In America
Land Art: A Complete Guide
The Art of Richard Long
Richard Long: Pocket Guide
Land Art In the UK
Land Art in Close-Up
Land Art In the U.S.A.
Land Art: Pocket Guide
Installation Art in Close-Up
Minimal Art and Artists In the 1960s and After
Colourfield Painting
Land Art DVD, TV documentary
Andy Goldsworthy DVD, TV documentary
The Erotic Object: Sexuality in Sculpture From Prehistory to the Present Day
Sex in Art: Pornography and Pleasure in Painting and Sculpture
Postwar Art
Sacred Gardens: The Garden in Myth, Religion and Art
Glorification: Religious Abstraction in Renaissance and 20th Century Art
Early Netherlandish Painting
Leonardo da Vinci
Piero della Francesca
Giovanni Bellini
Fra Angelico: Art and Religion in the Renaissance
Mark Rothko: The Art of Transcendence
Frank Stella: American Abstract Artist
Jasper Johns
Brice Marden
Alison Wilding: The Embrace of Sculpture
Vincent van Gogh: Visionary Landscapes
Eric Gill: Nuptials of God
Constantin Brancusi: Sculpting the Essence of Things
Max Beckmann
Caravaggio
Gustave Moreau
Egon Schiele: Sex and Death In Purple Stockings
Delizioso Fotografico Fervore: Works In Process 1
Sacro Cuore: Works In Process 2
The Light Eternal: J.M.W. Turner
The Madonna Glorified: Karen Arthurs

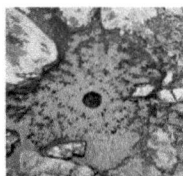

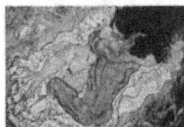

LITERATURE

J.R.R. Tolkien: The Books, The Films, The Whole Cultural Phenomenon
J.R.R. Tolkien: Pocket Guide
Tolkien's Heroic Quest
The *Earthsea* Books of Ursula Le Guin
Beauties, Beasts and Enchantment: Classic French Fairy Tales
German Popular Stories by the Brothers Grimm
Philip Pullman and *His Dark Materials*
Sexing Hardy: Thomas Hardy and Feminism
Thomas Hardy's *Tess of the d'Urbervilles*
Thomas Hardy's *Jude the Obscure*
Thomas Hardy: The Tragic Novels
Love and Tragedy: Thomas Hardy
The Poetry of Landscape in Hardy
Wessex Revisited: Thomas Hardy and John Cowper Powys
Wolfgang Iser: Essays and Interviews
Petrarch, Dante and the Troubadours
Maurice Sendak and the Art of Children's Book Illustration
Andrea Dworkin
Cixous, Irigaray, Kristeva: The *Jouissance* of French Feminism
Julia Kristeva: Art, Love, Melancholy, Philosophy, Semiotics and Psychoanalysis
Hélene Cixous I Love You: The *Jouissance* of Writing
Luce Irigaray: Lips, Kissing, and the Politics of Sexual Difference
Peter Redgrove: Here Comes the Flood
Peter Redgrove: Sex-Magic-Poetry-Cornwall
Lawrence Durrell: Between Love and Death, East and West
Love, Culture & Poetry: Lawrence Durrell
Cavafy: Anatomy of a Soul
German Romantic Poetry: Goethe, Novalis, Heine, Hölderlin
Feminism and Shakespeare
Shakespeare: Love, Poetry & Magic
The Passion of D.H. Lawrence
D.H. Lawrence: Symbolic Landscapes
D.H. Lawrence: Infinite Sensual Violence
Rimbaud: Arthur Rimbaud and the Magic of Poetry
The Ecstasies of John Cowper Powys
Sensualism and Mythology: The Wessex Novels of John Cowper Powys
Amorous Life: John Cowper Powys and the Manifestation of Affectivity (H.W. Fawkner)
Postmodern Powys: New Essays on John Cowper Powys (Joe Boulter)
Rethinking Powys: Critical Essays on John Cowper Powys
Paul Bowles & Bernardo Bertolucci
Rainer Maria Rilke
Joseph Conrad: *Heart of Darkness*
In the Dim Void: Samuel Beckett
Samuel Beckett Goes into the Silence
André Gide: Fiction and Fervour
Jackie Collins and the Blockbuster Novel
Blinded By Her Light: The Love-Poetry of Robert Graves
The Passion of Colours: Travels In Mediterranean Lands
Poetic Forms

POETRY

Ursula Le Guin: Walking In Cornwall
Peter Redgrove: Here Comes The Flood
Peter Redgrove: Sex-Magic-Poetry-Cornwall
Dante: Selections From the Vita Nuova
Petrarch, Dante and the Troubadours
William Shakespeare: Sonnets
William Shakespeare: Complete Poems
Blinded By Her Light: The Love-Poetry of Robert Graves
Emily Dickinson: Selected Poems
Emily Brontë: Poems
Thomas Hardy: Selected Poems
Percy Bysshe Shelley: Poems
John Keats: Selected Poems
Joh n Keats: Poems of 1820
D.H. Lawrence: Selected Poems
Edmund Spenser: Poems
Edmund Spenser: Amoretti
John Donne: Poems
Henry Vaughan: Poems
Sir Thomas Wyatt: Poems
Robert Herrick: Selected Poems
Rilke: Space, Essence and Angels in the Poetry of Rainer Maria Rilke
Rainer Maria Rilke: Selected Poems
Friedrich Hölderlin: Selected Poems
Arseny Tarkovsky: Selected Poems
Arthur Rimbaud: Selected Poems
Arthur Rimbaud: A Season in Hell
Arthur Rimbaud and the Magic of Poetry
Novalis: Hymns To the Night
German Romantic Poetry
Paul Verlaine: Selected Poems
Elizaethan Sonnet Cycles
D.J. Enright: By-Blows
Jeremy Reed: Brigitte's Blue Heart
Jeremy Reed: Claudia Schiffer's Red Shoes
Gorgeous Little Orpheus
Radiance: New Poems
Crescent Moon Book of Nature Poetry
Crescent Moon Book of Love Poetry
Crescent Moon Book of Mystical Poetry
Crescent Moon Book of Elizabethan Love Poetry
Crescent Moon Book of Metaphysical Poetry
Crescent Moon Book of Romantic Poetry
Pagan America: New American Poetry

MEDIA, CINEMA, FEMINISM and CULTURAL STUDIES

J.R.R. Tolkien: The Books, The Films, The Whole Cultural Phenomenon
J.R.R. Tolkien: Pocket Guide
The Lord of the Rings Movies: Pocket Guide
The Cinema of Hayao Miyazaki
Hayao Miyazaki: Princess Mononoke: Pocket Movie Guide
Hayao Miyazaki: Spirited Away: Pocket Movie Guide
Tim Burton : Hallowe'en For Hollywood
Ken Russell
Ken Russell: Tommy: Pocket Movie Guide
The Ghost Dance: The Origins of Religion
The Peyote Cult
Cixous, Irigaray, Kristeva: The Jouissance of French Feminism
Julia Kristeva: Art, Love, Melancholy, Philosophy, Semiotics and Psychoanalysis
Luce Irigaray: Lips, Kissing, and the Politics of Sexual Difference
Hélene Cixous I Love You: The Jouissance of Writing
Andrea Dworkin
'Cosmo Woman': The World of Women's Magazines
Women in Pop Music
HomeGround: The Kate Bush Anthology
Discovering the Goddess (Geoffrey Ashe)
The Poetry of Cinema
The Sacred Cinema of Andrei Tarkovsky
Andrei Tarkovsky: Pocket Guide
Andrei Tarkovsky: Mirror: Pocket Movie Guide
Andrei Tarkovsky: The Sacrifice: Pocket Movie Guide
Walerian Borowczyk: Cinema of Erotic Dreams
Jean-Luc Godard: The Passion of Cinema
Jean-Luc Godard: Hail Mary: Pocket Movie Guide
Jean-Luc Godard: Contempt: Pocket Movie Guide
Jean-Luc Godard: Pierrot le Fou: Pocket Movie Guide
John Hughes and Eighties Cinema
Ferris Bueller's Day Off: Pocket Movie Guide
Jean-Luc Godard: Pocket Guide
The Cinema of Richard Linklater
Liv Tyler: Star In Ascendance
Blade Runner and the Films of Philip K. Dick
Paul Bowles and Bernardo Bertolucci
Media Hell: Radio, TV and the Press
An Open Letter to the BBC
Detonation Britain: Nuclear War in the UK
Feminism and Shakespeare
Wild Zones: Pornography, Art and Feminism
Sex in Art: Pornography and Pleasure in Painting and Sculpture
Sexing Hardy: Thomas Hardy and Feminism

The Light Eternal is a model monograph, an exemplary job. The subject matter of the book is beautifully
organised and dead on beam. (Lawrence Durrell)
It is amazing for me to see my work treated with such passion and respect. (Andrea Dworkin)

CRESCENT MOON PUBLISHING
P.O. Box 1312, Maidstone, Kent, ME14 5XU, Great Britain. www.crmoon.com

cresmopub@yahoo.co.uk   www.crescentmoon.org.uk

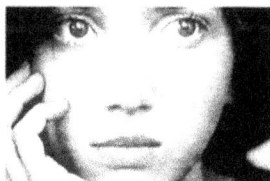

www.ingramcontent.com/pod-product-compliance
Lightning Source LLC
Chambersburg PA
CBHW060031050426
42448CB00012B/2953